What Human Resources Professionals Need to Stop Doing

Book 3 in the "Stop So You Can Get the Results You Want" Series

BY

LIZ WEBER, CMC, CSP

Also by Liz Weber, CMC, CSP

Something Needs to Change Around Here: The Five Stages to Leveraging Your Leadership

Don't Let 'Em Treat You Like a Girl: A Woman's Guide to Leadership Success

What Business Owners Need to Stop Doing

What Managers Need to Stop Doing

What Women in Leadership Need to Stop Doing

Stop So You Can Get The Results You Want

Special Offer

If you enjoyed Liz's insights in this book, take advantage of these special offers:

1. Take Liz's Free Leadership Assessment to determine which of The Five Stages of Focused Leadership® you are currently modeling! Just go to her website, wbsllc.com, to access the assessment!

2. Click here to download Liz's white paper featuring the three things you need to stop today! Go to www.wbsllc.com/stop-it/

Social Media

Visit my website: http://www.WBSLLC.com

Or connect with me on social media:

What Human Resources Professionals Need to Stop Doing

Book 3 in the "Stop So You Can Get the Results You Want" Series

By Liz Weber

Published 2019 by Aspen Hill Press

This book is licensed for your personal enjoyment and education only. While best efforts have been used, the author and publisher are not offering legal, accounting, medical, or any other professional services advice and make no representations or warranties of any kind and assume no liabilities of any kind with respect to the accuracy or completeness of the contents and specifically disclaim any implied warranties of merchantability or fitness of use for a particular purpose, nor shall they be held liable or responsible to any person or entity with respect to any loss or incidental or consequential damages caused, or alleged to have been caused, directly or indirectly, by the information or programs contained herein. Stories, characters, and entities are 'sanitized' versions of real client experiences.

The information in this book on personnel management is done in an informational manner only. All personnel actions should be reviewed carefully before implementation. Please consult with your human resources professionals, legal counsel etc before taking official action to ensure you are complying with company policies, as well as any and all state and federal employment laws.

All rights reserved. No part of this publication may be reproduced or transmitted in any form or by any means, electronic or mechanical, including photocopying, recording, or by any information storage and retrieval system, without permission in writing from the publisher. All images are free to use or share, even commercially, according to Google at the time of publication unless otherwise noted. Thank you for respecting the hard work of the author(s) and everyone else involved.

Copyright © 2019, 2015 by Liz Weber, Weber Business Services, LLC. All Rights Reserved.

Authors and sources cited throughout retain the copyright to their respective materials.

This book is dedicated to the thousands of human resources professionals I've had the pleasure of meeting and working with, but especially to the 323 who were surveyed for this project. Your job is truly challenging, yet so terribly important. I respect and appreciate the work you do.

Liz

"Change is inevitable, growth is optional."

John C. Maxwell

Contents

Introduction 1

{ 1 } Stop Thinking You're "Just HR" ___ 17

{ 2 } Stop Hiding in the Transactional _ 41

{ 3 } Stop Keeping What You Know and Do a Secret 59

{ 4 } Stop Talking Like HR _____ 75

{ 5 } Stop Negatively Branding HR ____ 95

{ 6 } Stop Saying "No" or "You Can't" as a First Response 109

{ 7 } Stop Giving Lip Service to Training and Coaching 119

{ 8 } Stop Acting Like a Cost Center Instead of a Value Center _____ 135

{ 9 } Stop Being a Weak Manager Yourself 157

Conclusion 193

Continue Your Leadership Journey ___ 199

About Liz Weber, CMC, CSP _____ 201

Introduction

"This whole game of business revolves around one thing: you build the best team, you win."

— Jack Welch, former CEO, General Electric

HELPING TO BUILD great teams is what human resources should be about. I start almost every speech I give to human resources professionals with the above quote by Jack Welch. But his quote doesn't go far enough. To build the best team, you need to recruit the right people, then on-board them correctly, then train them individually and collectively, then coach them when needed, then help them develop as productive team members and people, then challenge them to grow (individually and collectively) as your business changes and grows, all while engaging with them to help them share and give their best. Then and only then do you have a chance at retaining them as a high-functioning, effective team that will help you succeed and win.

Needless to say, that's not easy. It's especially difficult when most of these team building, employee development and training activities happen under the influence of other managers. Managers who are not skilled in or focused on employee or team development. For far too many managers, focusing on the "soft skills" is touchy-feely crap. However, this just reinforces the reality that your job is not only that of a supplier of quality workers to the workplace, but it also needs to be that of an advisor, coach, and trainer to management on how to develop the best teams... to win.

To serve this two-fold purpose, you need to harness your technical and interpersonal skills as a human resources professional. You've got to deal with all levels of staff within the organization: frontline staff and frontline supervisors, mid-level management and senior staff, C-suite executives and boards, and let's not forget the business owners and their family members.

It's not easy, but it can be terribly fun. Why? People are great, but people are also wacky. There are never any guarantees on how a manager or an employee will or won't respond, behave, or act. But it's up to you to be the guide and the internal source of reason, objectivity, and most of all, common sense when dealing with people within the organization.

It's up to you to be the guide and the internal source of reason, objectivity, and most of all, common sense when dealing with people within the organization.

Helping to develop people and build great teams is what human resources is all about, and building high-functioning teams is what leadership teams care about. So that's where you should be focusing your work for your company as a human resources professional: Give the leadership team what they really want, even if they don't realize they need it yet. Help them develop incredible team members and teams that can help the company now and that will be right for the company in the future.

The leadership team doesn't really care that you run payroll seamlessly or process all employees through open enrollment with minimal disruption to production; those outcomes are expected. From the leadership team's perspective, that's your department's bare minimum expected output. That's no different than expecting Marketing to ensure the right messaging is going out into the marketplace to reinforce the brand, the press releases are timely and relevant, and the website is promoting the right items at the right time to support the sales teams and production. So don't expect any kudos for doing your tactical HR functions. Those are appreciated and required. However, to be viewed as a respected key advisor and partner to management, you need to do more.

Focus your work as a human resources professional for your company on helping to build great teams. Give the other leaders what they really want, even if they don't realize it yet.

Now, I'm going to take you on a bit of a tangent here, but stay with me because these next few paragraphs share the overall concept of the book:

When working with clients on strategic planning, one of the first areas we cover is getting clarity on their market and customer base. In a nutshell, I need them to confirm they're actually targeting the right types of customers to allow them to be the type of business they want to be.

So how do my clients clarify whom they want to target? I have them determine whom they want as their customers. To do this, I have them review their current portfolio of customers. As they analyze their customers, I have them place each customer in one of four tiers:

Tier 1 Customers: These are their ideal and highly profitable customers. They excite and energize my clients. They bring new projects to my clients that keep my clients' businesses evolving by developing new services and products to meet their customers' and other customers' current and future needs.

Tier 2 Customers: These are their good income providers. These customers are content with my clients' core products and services. These customers make my clients feel as though they're in the right business because they can service these customers relatively easily and make a fair profit in doing so.

Tier 3 Customers: These customers create those break-even jobs for my clients and consume more than their fair share of my clients' time and materials. These customers frustrate my clients more often than they realize.

Tier 4 Customers: These customers cost my clients money. In fact, these customers frustrate my clients because they're never happy. They're not a fit for my clients and my clients are not a fit for them. Therefore, it's a painful relationship for everyone.

The gist of this exercise is for my clients to get clearer on whom they currently are serving and targeting and whom they should be serving and targeting. Most companies are spending a lot of time serving customers in Tiers 3 and 4, when they should be spending time with Tier 1 and 2 customers.

Most companies are spending a lot of time serving customers in Tiers 3 and 4, when they should be spending time with Tier 1 and 2 customers.

The Tier of the customer also aligns with how they, the customers, view and treat my clients:

Tier 1 customers view and treat my clients as *partners* who help them, the customers, improve their products, services, and businesses. These customers are looking to continue to build a long-term trusted relationship.

Tier 2 customers view and treat my clients as *advisors* who help them find answers to issues or needs. These customers are looking to continue seek my clients out as respected sources.

Tier 3 customers view and treat my clients as *problem-solvers* or *problem fixers*. "Here, take care of this. That's your job." These customers are looking for easy, efficient interactions and services.

Tier 4 customers view and treat my clients as *the cheapest source* or *only source*. They're also viewed as replaceable commodities. As soon as a Tier 4 customer can find a cheaper alternative source, they'll leave. They're not loyal. These types of customers are looking for immediate personal gain only.

Now here's the interesting part as it pertains to you as an HR professional. Your *internal* customers (the other managers and employees, and anyone within the organization who relies upon you for support and information) view and treat you as a Tier 1, 2, 3 or 4 customer, too. So the question becomes: *How do you get them to view and treat you as a Tier 1 or 2 customer—a trusted partner or advisor?*

You need to stop doing a few specific things. And I don't say that from my observations alone. A 2014 Deloitte study of executives found that less than 8% of the HR leaders surveyed believe their HR teams have the skills to meet their businesses' needs. In addition 48% of the respondents indicated that HR wasn't ready to reskill itself to meet the demands of global business. Given that, this book is intended to help you identify what you need to stop doing so you can start "reskilling" yourself, your team, and the HR function to better serve the needs of the organization going forward.

How do you get the leadership team to view you and treat you as their Human

Resources partner or advisor? Stop doing a few specific things.

I hope you find a few of the following ideas helpful. I hope you don't find them hurtful. Because I'm not a human resources professional, but am instead a management consultant, the ideas presented are from a consultant's perspective and not HR's perspective. So I may share a few things you believe are politically incorrect or insulting. That's not my intent. My intent is to make you aware of what others haven't. My intent is to help you be an even more knowledgeable and intentional human resources professional. So let's get started.

"Success in business is all about people, people, people. Whatever industry a company is in, its employees are its biggest competitive advantage."

— *Sir Richard Branson, founder, Virgin Group*

{ 1 } Stop Thinking You're "Just HR"

"We teach people how to treat us."

— *Dr. Phil McGraw, author, psychologist,*

television host

WHY: YOU ARE devaluing yourself and what you and your department do and what you can bring to the organization. When you say things such as, "I'm just HR," you devalue the role of human resources within your organization because you're guiding others in leadership to view you and the human resources function as some sort of second tier role—and then to treat you as such. You're also helping to perpetuate the limited perspective some managers have on what human resources is and does: *It's just the department that hires, fires, and pays employees.* These responsibilities alone are huge! They're incredibly important as they impact the workforce readiness, talent pool, morale, engagement, productivity, culture, and so on, whether they're done well or not. And that fact alone should cause every other manager to respect the work you do tremendously. However, by using the words "just HR," you're minimizing the value of these traditional, core HR functions.

To help you get beyond the 'just HR' mindset, let me share with you an insight and challenge I share with every human resources vice president, director, and manager I coach on a client's leadership team:

You and your department should be doing for your leadership team what you just hired me to do: Coach your management team to better understand what their real jobs are as leaders. Teach them how to behave as an effective leadership team. Teach them how to identify and tee-up for debate, approval, and action organizational initiatives. Help them develop stronger teams deep and enterprise-wide. Help them learn to better read and support their team members, clear roadblocks, and move your organization forward.

If you're focused on processing payroll, benefits enrollments, or something else important but tactical, you're not serving the leadership team or the organization as well as you could or should.

If you're focused on processing payroll, benefits enrollments, or something else important but tactical, you're not serving the leadership team or the organization as well as you could or should.

I'm also going to share something I don't typically share: You, along with many of the human resources professionals within my client organizations are better equipped to do what I do than I am:

- You know the direct daily impact of poor training and negative morale on your company's bottom line; I don't.
- You know the true leadership strengths and challenges of the organization's leaders; I don't.
- You know the internal politics, networks, hidden culture, and unspoken ambitions of the leaders; I don't.

Yet the leadership teams listen to me more readily. Why? I've not positioned myself as second-tier support to the leadership team. I've positioned myself as a leadership team advisor and partner because of the issues I raise with them and the ones I challenge them to address. I keep them focused on thinking and acting as leaders.

What do you need to start planning for and implementing now to ensure you've got a solid tomorrow? How can you develop stronger teams and build an even better company? What do you need to do to make that happen?

Honestly, much of what I walk the leadership team through is what human resources professionals are trained to do:

- Teach the leadership team how to hold everyone accountable to the values and to do the jobs they're being paid to do.
- Identify and plan for the organizational and workforce changes needed now and as the company will be in 3, 4, 5+ years.
- Create and update standard operational procedures (SOPs), polices, and other systems to enhance consistency, support cross-training, and develop a company knowledge bank.

- Create a culture of knowledge sharing, team development, and continual learning.
- Develop performance management systems and processes that enhance clarity, transparency, and relationships.
- Develop an ongoing leadership and employee development process to make things stick.

I keep the leadership team focused on building a better company and being better leaders. When it's leadership strategy time, I don't allow them to get lost in the details of one specific project, one specific employee, or one specific issue. I cause them to think bigger, more impactful, more strategic.

As I said earlier, if you continue to position yourself as "just HR," you will continue to be consulted only when other leaders want you to hire, fire, pay or provide benefits to someone. If you want to be consulted on more impactful and strategic issues, position yourself as the leadership team's advisor and partner because of what you force them to focus on as leaders. Show them how you can help them do their jobs even better.

Position yourself as the leadership team's advisor and partner because of what you force them to focus on as leaders.

As I walked to the conference room to kick-off a multi-year leadership planning and development project with a client, Heidi, the HR manager, said:

"Liz, I really hope you can get the senior team to focus because I can't. They don't listen to me. I'm the newbie manager here, and besides, I'm just HR. These guys have known each other for years. They've got their own way of doing things, and that's not necessarily good. They

don't stay focused on anything strategic for long. As a leadership team, we don't focus on the right things. We drift and end up discussing specific projects. We don't attack the big issues we know we have that are affecting our employees. We need to do a better job for our managers and employees."

In that one commentary, Heidi had summed up the leadership team's fundamental problems. She knew what they were:

- They didn't think and act as a senior leadership team should.

- They didn't hold themselves accountable to be stronger leaders for their managers and employees.
- They didn't focus and act on strategic issues to move the organization and employees forward.

Even though Heidi had correctly identified the leadership team's issues, she had negated her ability as a member of the leadership team to do anything about them.

However, as the strategic planning session progressed it became frustratingly obvious that again Heidi was right: the other managers on the leadership team didn't listen to her. To be honest, if I had been in their place, I wouldn't have either. Of all the senior leaders sitting around that conference table, Heidi was the one who spoke the least. When she did speak, she spoke with little conviction, she quickly backed away from her opinions, and appeared the least knowledgeable about the business and specific challenges the other department heads faced. She continued to position herself not only as the newest member to the management team, but as the weakest.

In listening to Heidi's comments to the group, it was obvious she didn't hold her position, responsibilities, or authority up to the same level of importance and respect as the production manager's, or the transportation manager's, or the finance manager's. She kept making comments such as, "I understand this is more challenging in your department, however..." or, " I know I don't have the headaches you have because I only have a handful of employees, but..." or "I don't know when we would be up to do that, we're so busy in HR."

Each time she'd make one of these comments, I would cringe. Each time she'd make one of these comments, the other managers would spend even less time listening to her or looking at her. It was like watching an automobile accident happen in slow motion:

Heidi kept diminishing her own credibility. It was a scenario I had seen too many times before: The head of human resources was reinforcing the perception to the rest of the management team that she and her department were... just HR.

About mid-way through the first work session, the team was discussing key positions within the organization. The president of the company asked, "Liz from your experience with other companies, what position or what departments should really be key in supporting the president? Which position sitting around this table, should I be listening to more? I know which one I think it is, but I'd like to hear what your experience has been." From the conversation leading up to his question I knew he was expecting and somewhat hoping that I would say the CFO. Instead, when I said, "Human Resources," and pointed to Heidi, his eyebrows raised in shock. The other managers around the table looked at me in stunned silence.

Because I'd completely surprised them with my answer, I simply looked at them for about 15 seconds so they understood I wasn't joking. Once they knew I was serious, I explained to them, as I already mentioned in this book's introduction, the human resources function should be doing for them what I was doing for them. Because of the training and experiences of that role, that position should be best poised to advise the president and other members of the leadership team on where the best talent is within the organization and how to best leverage and enhance those skills. Ensuring you've got the right people, with the right skills, in the right spots, at the right time is critical for success. And that's what HR does in collaboration with the leadership team.

Now, I have to give the president of the company and the other members of the leadership team credit because no one laughed or said, "Yeah right," or was otherwise disrespectful to Heidi. However, it was a watershed moment for them and for her. They all realized human resources had a bigger role to play in that company.

HR is the position best poised to advise the president and other members of the leadership team on where the best talent is within the organization and how to best leverage and enhance those skills.

After several work sessions with the team, and coaching sessions with Heidi, her mindset changed from pigeon-holing herself as "just HR", to the understanding that—as a manager and member of the leadership team—she and her department needed to do more with the human resources function and responsibilities.

As a result of her mindset—and behavior changes—Heidi made several intentional changes. She outsourced or delegated numerous tasks that did not require her individual or her small team's time and talent to do. She started interacting more as a peer with the other managers. She started asking deeper questions about their departments, about their staffing concerns, and about their department needs for the future. She started raising issues during management meetings about the need to intentionally—and as a team—plan for a stronger, better-trained workforce. She pushed for select initiatives and not surprisingly, she was told, "If you think they're important, then you make them happen." She did.

Needless to say, Heidi's mindset and behavior changes, caused the other managers to view and treat her differently. They now look to her as not only a respected peer, but also as an advisor and partner in moving the company forward.

Here's what I suggest you do instead: Recognize your department, your role, and you are more than "just HR." What the Human Resources Department and you can bring to the leadership team, the employees, and the future of the company is huge! It's time to show it and share it.

Take dedicated steps to learn more about organizational growth and development. Understand its value to a leadership team. Deconstruct organizational initiatives that have occurred in your organization, and uncover why some succeeded and others failed. Decipher what role stronger leadership planning, communication, or action could have played in changing the outcome.

Make efforts to learn more about the other departments. Spend time with the other managers learning about them, their departmental challenges, their leadership challenges, and their personal strengths and challenges. Identify small ways you can help them do their jobs more effectively. Position yourself so you are more aware of planned or needed adjustments in organizational structure, staffing, and skill sets so you can best support the other managers proactively in moving the organization to where it needs to go.

Finally, start to intentionally position yourself as an internal consultant, advisor, and coach to other managers to support them in better working with, developing, and teaming with their employees. Become their partner and the internal expert on organizational development and talent management.

"The [CHRO] should be a key sparring partner for the CEO on topics like talent development, team composition, [and] managing culture."

— *Thomas Ebeling, CEO, ProSiebenSat.1 Media AG*

{ 2 } Stop Hiding in the Transactional

"HR departments around the world are viewed as having lower analytical skills than other departments, leaving them ill-prepared for the era of 'big data.'"

—*2013 Global Study, American Management Association*

WHY: THE TRANSACTIONAL is replaceable. The transactional responsibilities of Human Resources (payroll and benefits administration, and so on) can be outsourced relatively easily. Though they are incredibly important and are needed to support the employees as well as management, the transactional can, for the most part, be completed by a software program or two. When what you do can easily be replaced by a computer application or piece of machinery, your value to the organization obviously drops.

When what you do can easily be replaced by a computer application or piece of machinery, your value to the organization obviously drops.

Also, when you make the basic transactional tasks you're responsible for sound more difficult than they actually are or should be, your management skills are put in question by the other members of the leadership team. They question your ability to take on and handle anything of greater importance or value. They also see what you don't: You're holding on tightly to doing things the way they've always been done, instead of doing things more efficiently.

You're holding on tightly to doing things the way they've always been done, instead of doing things more efficiently.

Also, I'm going to be honest with you, the leadership team doesn't really care that you and your team seamlessly processed payroll for 500 employees while you also completed open enrollment for everyone with minimal disruption to production. The leadership team isn't impressed and they really don't want to hear about it. Those functions are expected of the human resources department. The leadership team will be grateful, but they won't be impressed. Again, those outputs are expected. They're expected to be done either by your team or by a third party vendor. The leadership team doesn't care how they get done. The leadership team just wants them done efficiently and without problems so you and they can focus on more important issues.

Finally, if you spend your time, energy, and focusing capabilities processing transactional items, you're not spending your time, energy, and focusing capabilities on more valuable, more strategic things; things that can actually help move the organization forward. To be blunt, you're also performing at a support staff level instead of key advisor level.

To be a partner and key advisor to the leadership team, you need to focus on the right issues, tasks, and data. If you're time is consumed with the transactional duties, you're not focusing on strategic issues such as: *Are we getting the right people trained for the right positions at the right time?* If your time is focused mostly on the transactional data (such as how quickly and accurately open enrollment was managed), you're not focusing on the organizationally impactful data: *How quickly and effectively are we on-boarding new employees?* As the quote at the start of this chapter alludes, human resources professionals are not ready, or not viewed as ready, to manage the data that's available to them in a way that matters to leaders.

Human resources professionals are not ready, or not viewed as ready, to manage the data that's available to them in a way that matters to leaders.

Let's make sure that statement doesn't apply to you. To do that, you need be able to focus on the right issues and data so you can provide management insights into what the workforce data is indicating. That type of insight helps you help the leadership team make key workforce and organizational decisions sooner rather than later, and that's what the leadership team needs and appreciates.

As I was preparing for a client's leadership training session to start, Bill, the human resources manager, walked into the training room and said, "Liz I'm sorry, but I'm going to have to miss training today. I've got to process payroll this afternoon, and if I don't do it right, I'm going to have 350 very angry production employees standing outside my office later!" He actually seemed a bit pleased with himself at the importance of the duty he was about to undertake.

I was both surprised and confused as to why Bill was processing the payroll himself, and also why the company was still processing it internally. So when I asked Bill these questions, he looked at me with a bit of bravado and said, "Well you see Liz, our payroll is very complicated." Because I'm not an expert in payroll processing I asked him in all honesty, "Why is it so complicated?" I have to be honest, I could tell Bill was now getting a bit frustrated with me but he humored me and replied, "We have a complicated process I have to follow to ensure it's done correctly. I also triple check every number and every calculation to make sure I'm being fair to the employees and to make sure I'm being fair to the company. I've been doing this for almost 30 years and if there's one thing I've learned, it's that accuracy now will save me a lot of time later when we file the payroll taxes."

Now, by this point in our conversation, I was intentionally pushing Bill's buttons a bit, when I said, "Bill, I'm sorry but I still don't understand why your payroll should so complicated that you need to spend *your* time processing it. You've got 350 production employees and 50 salaried staff. That's not a unique payroll structure." Bill controlled himself as he replied, "It's how I've always done it, and I don't trust anyone else to do it correctly. I need to get the process started." and he left.

Later that afternoon I was talking with Carla, the president of the company, about various leadership concerns I had given some of the conversations during training. I also shared with her the gist of the conversation I'd had with Bill prior to training. Carla looked at me, pursed her lips, and said:

"You're right. I know. Bill has control issues about payroll. He makes such a big deal out of it. He won't let anyone else handle it. If he's sick, he'll still come into work and do it. He even came into work the morning of a family funeral to process payroll! It's weird I know, but it's not been high on my priority list. He does it. It's done right. There are no complaints. I've let it go. I guess I need to do something about it."

As I was leaving Carla's office, Bill walked up to me and asked, "May I speak with you for a moment?" When we had gone into Bill's office and he closed the door, Bill said, "Liz, I've never before had to explain out loud why I process payroll the way I do. But earlier, when I heard myself explaining my rationale to you, I heard how stupid it was! I've been holding on to doing this task because I've always done it. I created the process and I can do it fairly quickly and accurately. But I'm embarrassed to say, I finally realize I do it because it's what I've always done!"

Within a few short months Bill had outsourced the payroll responsibility to a third-party vendor. In talking with him about the transition, I asked him what he was doing with his time instead of processing payroll. He smiled and said:

"My team and I have been getting training and support from the payroll company on how to use the data they provide in their payroll reports. With their help, we're creating a dashboard of key metrics we can use here to support the leadership team. For instance, we identified a potential retirement bubble of almost 30% of our workforce in five years! Because of that, I've been talking with the other managers and we've already put a few things in place to handle it. For instance, my team is working with the various managers in identifying what key processes need to be documented or cross-

trained, so we don't have knowledge walking out the door with the retirees. This whole thing is still a work in process and I still am learning, but I can tell I'm personally doing things that matter to the company."

Here's what I suggest you do instead: Review your personal work habits as well as the overall human resources operations. Identify what tasks and processes could be better served by others or by outsourcing them—freeing you and your staff up to do more mission-focused, productive work.

If you, like a participant on one of my webinars, are concerned that you will be faced with resistance by the leadership team if you suggest outsourcing some of the transactional tasks, conduct a basic cost/benefit analysis. Contact three to five vendors and ask them to provide proposals to justify their taking over select tasks. Have them help you rationalize and justify the expense of paying money to a third-party provider versus doing the tasks in-house. If the results of the bids indicate it makes not only productive, but also financial sense to outsource the tasks, make your case to the owner, CEO, or leadership team. If it doesn't, identify ways to perform the tasks even more efficiently.

Continue to position yourself as a leadership team advisor. Be proactive and make the leadership team aware of industry trends and technologies you're monitoring for possible impact and/or implementation within your organization. Ensure the leadership team is informed to make proactive decisions wisely and that maximize ROI. Your expertise and insights will be appreciated, and the entire organization will benefit.

Be proactive and make the leadership team aware of industry trends and technologies you're monitoring for possible impact and/or implementation within your organization.

When you're so busy being busy with the transactional, you don't have the mental free space or the physical capacity to take on more or to think strategically. Therefore, you need to either delegate to others within HR or you need to outsource what can be capably handled by a third-party vendor or vendors specializing in specific HR support. In a nutshell, ensure you're serving the organization as you can most effectively, and that you are doing the job you're being paid to do.

> *"The question isn't who is going to let me; it's who is going to stop me."*
>
> — *Ayn Rand, author and philosopher*

{ 3 } Stop Keeping What You Know and Do a Secret

"Tell the negative committee who meets inside your head to sit down and be quiet."

— *Gloria Wilson, painter and social media personality*

WHY: IF PEOPLE don't know what you do, they won't value your role and your work. If you want a respected seat at the leadership table, you have to earn it and then regularly demonstrate, through your actions and words, why you have the right to keep it.

If you want a respected seat at the leadership table, you have to earn it and then regularly demonstrate, through your actions and words, why you have the right to keep it.

It's a behavior all too common in many managers—the resistance to talk about what they do well for fear of appearing boastful. Yet, as noted in the previous chapter, many well-intentioned managers readily share how hard they work on transactional tasks, only to have the members of their leadership teams not care. So what are you supposed to do? How can you avoid this dilemma? Identify what matters. Do what matters. Report on what matters.

Identify what matters. Do what matters. Report on what matters.

During a keynote speech, I was sharing this idea with a large group of human resources professionals, when I noticed a woman sitting close to the stage start to shake her head. I asked if she had a question or counter thought, and she replied, "Liz, I'm not dumb, but I don't know what matters. I just do what needs to be done. How am I supposed to report on what matters if I don't know what the management team wants, because they don't even know what they want!"

Several other audience members cheered and started to clap in agreement with her. So I shared with them a basic process I created to help my business clients get clearer on what value they bring to their customers, so they can better articulate their value to their targeted customers. The same process works for human resources professionals in articulating their value to the leadership team and others within the organization.

The exercise is called *Because of You...* and the rationale behind it is that people appreciate others who help them move forward or otherwise improve. So to help the leadership team understand how you help them now or how you can help them if they work more closely with you, you need to be able to clarify for them how you can move them forward. You need to clarify how you will help them transition from the state they were in to the improved state they want to get to.

To do this, simply complete the following phrases as if you were a member or members of your leadership team. Channel what you think they could or should say as a result of the types of things you've helped them do or achieve. Given the objective of many of your HR initiatives (objective employee actions, quicker more effective employee on-boarding, effective coaching with managers on better performance management techniques, clearer leadership communications focused management of projects you initiated, and so on), what outcomes have they realized?

Simply fill in the blanks as a member or members of the leadership team would)

Because of working with (your name)/ Human Resources...

- I/we (the leadership team) no longer:

- I/we can now:

- I/we know how to:

- I/we are able to

- I/we now have:

- I/we will:

- I/we will be able to:

Here's an example of how someone in your position might complete these phrases:

- I/we (the leadership team) no longer *have excessive employee turnover.*

- I/we can now *more quickly on-board new team members and get them productive quicker.*

- I/we know how to *quickly and objectively make team members aware of unacceptable behaviors.*

- I/we are able to *manage projects more effectively and profitably.*

- I/we now have *team members offering ideas and solving problems instead of just the management team doing so.*

- I/we will *be able to delegate more effectively and develop even more team members.*

- I/we will be able to *spend more time planning for the future knowing my team is handling daily operations.*

In reviewing the sample above, can you see how valuable you are and what your department does for other managers and the organization? Did you also notice how the phrases transition from the past through the present to the future? You've helped transition a manager or managers from a prior state to a better future state.

You've helped transition a manager or managers from a prior state to a better future state.

By providing training and coaching to managers, you've helped them to interact more effectively with employees and you've reduced turnover. By working closely with the various department managers, your team helped enhance the new employee on-boarding process and initial departmental training processes. By teaching managers how to more comfortably deal with unacceptable behaviors, you've helped them to more quickly address issues before they get out of control. By spearheading the project management training project, you've helped all managers and key project managers learn how to more effectively manage projects and project teams. By working with the managers and employees on innovation and problem solving, you've helped to increase the number of employees identifying and sharing process improvement ideas. And by coordinating the leadership training programs that shared insights with the managers, they're now able to delegate more effectively and spend their time focusing on what they need to be focusing their time and energy on. By doing your job, you've added value. It's time to let others know about it and stop keeping it a secret.

It's time to let others know what you do and the value you bring. Stop keeping it a secret.

Here's what I suggest you do instead: Complete the exercise above with at least 2-3 examples for each phrase. Ideally, have 4-5 examples for each phrase. If you have a hard time completing the phrases, it's time to start to identify for yourself and others your value. This activity alone should help you better appreciate what value you bring to the managers, the leadership team, the employees and the organization.

Next, develop a list of the various human resources programs, initiatives, services, and activities you and your team provide or have provided. Once the list is developed, identify the benefits others realized or derive from those programs, initiatives, services and activities. Clarify how others have or do benefit from your work.

Review those lists and give yourself a well-deserved pat on the back for the value you bring to the organization. But then, take intentional steps to clarify for the leadership team what value you and human resources bring to them, their departments, their employees, and the organization. Be ready to communicate the beneficial impact of your training initiatives. Clarify the positive results on turnover and employee actions because of your coaching and webinars. Stay on top of the current data that continues to validate the effectiveness of your efforts to help employee innovation. Stay on top of the data and be ready to share it—not to tout your achievements—but to validate you and your department's value and your right to be a key advisor, partner, and leader.

Remember, you need to identify what matters. Do what matters. Report on what matters. That's how you maintain your right to be a key advisor and partner.

Stay on top of the data and be ready to share it—not to tout your achievements—but to validate you and your department's value and your right to be a key advisor, partner, and leader.

"If you have an important point to make, don't try to be subtle or clever. Use a pile driver. Hit the point once. Then come back and hit it again. Then hit it a third time—a tremendous whack."

— *Winston Churchill, Former Prime Minister of the United Kingdom*

{ 4 } Stop Talking Like HR

"Good communication is as stimulating as black coffee, and just as hard to sleep after."

— *Anne Morrow Lindbergh, author*

WHY: WHEN YOU use organizational development and human resources-specific terms frequently in your communications, you run the risk of 'turning off' other members of the leadership team who don't understand or appreciate them. As a result, they may well assume you are once again speaking about "fluffy, cumbersome HR things" that might make people feel good, require a lot of paperwork, and do nothing to move the organization. With that as their mindset, it's difficult for you and the work you do to be valued or supported. Therefore, you need to learn to speak in a way they'll understand and appreciate.

In Chapter 1, I shared just one client example that indicated the CEO viewed the CFO as his most trusted advisor and senior team member. I'm comfortable saying from my experience, that's a common mindset and behavior of many CEOs. Also, typically and understandably so, the CEO and CFO are the two positions that hold the most decision making and budget authority for many organizations. And, let's not forget, that in far too many organizations, human resources reports to the CFO, because it's viewed as a cost center.

Therefore, if you want to get leadership support and financial backing for new initiatives or continued support for current programs, you need to communicate in terms the CEO, CFO, and other members of the management team will understand. You need to speak less with HR terms and speak more with financial terms.

If you want to get leadership support and financial backing for new initiatives or continued support for current programs, you need to communicate in terms the CEO, CFO, and other members of the management team will understand.

Now that may sound a bit unfair and demeaning to your profession and expertise, but if the overwhelming majority of management teams across the business world speak the financial language of business, doesn't it make sense that you should learn to speak that language too? Instead of speaking in HR terms, speak in financial business terms to clarify what you do, what you propose, what you mean, how you add value, the results of your work, the impact on production, the impact on the employee population, and the impact on the bottom line.

When you can more clearly communicate what you do, want, and need in financial terms, your success with various employee engagement initiatives you've tracked with your human capital metrics can be more readily understood by CEOs and CFOs with budget authority. By communicating in terms CEOs, CFOs, and other leaders can understand, you can more strategically drive conversations and decisions about your organization's human resources.

In 2014, the staffing service Accountemps conducted a survey of U.S. and Canadian based human resources managers and asked them to identify the most annoying business words. The results of the survey included these all too common human resources terms:

- Paradigm shift
- Deep dive
- Synergy
- Core competency
- Employee engagement

If these terms irritate HR professionals, how do you think non-HR managers feel when they hear them? I expect they tune them, and you, out.

Speak less with HR terms and speak more with financial terms.

I recently facilitated a strategic planning session in which Paul, the Director of Human Resources, was an active participant. However, he'd say things such as:

"We need to ensure we're continuously creating a safe, supportive, and engaging environment to promote the open exchange of ideas among our associates while driving home

the idea of self-empowerment and accountability. That is the type of transformational change we're trying to achieve here."

Needless to say, I'd see the other managers look at him, squint a bit as they tried to process what he had just said, and then look back at me. So, I'd rephrase his comment. "Good. You want to change the environment here to one in which every employee realizes they're expected to contribute, yet they feel supported and comfortable sharing their ideas. Did I understand you correctly?" The managers, including Paul, would nod as their eyes lit up: "Yes! That's what we want!" After the third time I rephrased one of his comments, I caught myself thinking to myself, "Paul, if that's what you meant, then say that! Speak in basic terms every manager without an HR certification will understand."

After that work session, I asked Paul to stay for a few minutes so we could talk. During that day's work session, several major initiatives had been discussed that would require substantial leadership by Paul and his team.

"Paul, thank you for sharing your insights and ideas today. It's obvious to me you understand, at a strategic level, what needs to happen here to take this organization to the next level."

Paul replied, "Yeah, I'm excited about our future. It's going to be a challenging but critical time for us. We've worked hard over the past five years to put some key transformational pieces into play. We need to implement the next phase well too."

"May I offer you some unsolicited leadership advice?"

Paul suddenly, looked a bit hesitant, but said, "Sure."

I responded:

"Don't hide your brilliance behind confusing HR terms. Every idea you shared today, every caution you highlighted, and every insight into the company's organizational dynamics were

critical to the team's decision-making today. But you tend to speak to this team as you do to your HR team. You use HR buzzwords that don't resonate with the other mangers. Did you notice they'd look at me to translate for you? That's not fair to you and that's not fair to them.

Speak to them in terms they'll understand and support. If even two of the initiatives discussed today are approved on the final plan, you'll need all the support from them you can get. Speak to them so they can understand and help you. You'll gain even more respect from them if you do."

He did and they did.

Here's what I suggest you do instead: First—Take a deep dive and identify your core competencies that will enable you to effectively lead a paradigm shift to enhance synergies across departments and also increase employee engagement. (Sorry I couldn't help myself. It was too easy!)

Second—Listen to how your management colleagues speak. Pay attention to how managers throughout the organization speak. Note which terms resonate with them and which don't. Identify what key metrics cause them to focus harder, ask more questions, get anxious or relax. Then, start to use those terms and metrics in how you communicate the work you do, the programs you are proposing, or the support from them you need and why.

Third—Ensure you understand the Key Performance Indicators (KPIs) your organization's leadership team focuses on and tracks. The KPIs are the critical metrics the senior team members focus on, as they're the measuring stick for project and performance success or failure. You need to understand what causes upticks or downturns in the KPIs so you better understand the overall business.

Fourth—Include stories and analogies to better explain and draw a picture of what you're trying to communicate. Even in the business world, people are people and human beings tend to pay attention to, remember, and relate to stories. So as you share ideas or propose new initiatives, use your skills in dealing with people to help others understand you better. Share examples of how specific actions will impact an employee class or department. Share how other organizations are effectively doing what you're suggesting. Help the other mangers see images in their mind through stories.

Fifth—As you use the workforce analytics available to you, identify which data points should be connected to share a potential scenario or tell a bigger story, and which should be placed aside for the time being. Don't just regurgitate the data. You need to be able to explain it and tell why the data matters to the leadership team. You need to be the expert on explaining the HR metrics in financial terms, while also sharing employee or department case-based examples, so your HR perspective, request, or proposal resonates with the CEO, CFO, and others on the leadership team.

If your analytics are projecting a retirement bubble starting in three years, your insight is needed to extrapolate that to: "Because our data are showing we have a very real potential 30% retirement bubble that will impact our workforce starting in 3 years and running for 4 years after that, we need to take action now. In two departments immediately and also company-wide, we need to start ensuring that those prospective retirees' knowledge is being shared, cross-trained to others, and captured. Otherwise, John, you're going to have a serious problem in Shipping and Mikka, you're going to be in trouble in Accounting." That scenario has impact.

Sixth—Get better at reading the environment and person or people with whom you're interacting. If you're one-on-one with an employee or manager who simply needs your time and insight, sit back and talk. Have a conversation. Be there for them. However, when it's time to be the representative for human resources, especially when you're at the leadership table or interacting with another member of the leadership team, be comfortable being direct and concise. Intentionally get to the main point without the background information. If others want more information, they'll ask for it.

Finally—Take time to learn the basics of finance. This insight will help you better understand the financial and the business-side of your business, but it will also enable you to then understand, analyze and comment on both the financial side and the people side of decisions coming before the leadership team.

This suggestion is big. Ask your leadership team CFO, Comptroller, Accounting Manager or colleague to help you understand the basic financial terms, ratios, or Key Performance Indicators (KPIs) that should matter to you and HR, that matter to the other mangers, and that matter to the leadership team. Don't be embarrassed. Ask. I've long since stopped being amazed at the number of senior leaders who don't understand the financial metrics shared with them regularly. So ask. You'll gain greater respect from your financial colleagues by being honest and willing to learn, and you'll enhance your own skill sets in the process.

You need to be the expert on explaining the HR metrics in financial terms, so your

HR perspective, request, or proposal resonates with the CEO, CFO, and others on the leadership team.

"The two words information and communication are often used interchangeably, but they signify quite different things. Information is giving out; communication is getting through."

— Sydney Harris, Journalist

{ 5 } Stop Negatively Branding HR

"Sometimes people treat us the way they do, not because of the way they are, but because of the way we are."

— Sam Horn, author, Tongue Fu!

WHY: IF YOU want to be treated like a partner and advisor to employees and management alike, act like one. If you want to be treated like a disciplinarian or bureaucratic roadblock, act like one.

In far too many organizations, the employees view the human resources department as the place they have to go when they're in trouble. It's reminiscent of being sent to the principal's office. "Uh oh. You're in trouble now!"

Similarly, in far too many organizations, managers view the human resources department as a necessary evil. To them, it's reminiscent of having to deal with a governmental bureaucracy: Nothing is easy; everything involves paperwork and regulations; you're treated as an interruption; and the final answer is often 'No.'

If you want to be treated like a partner and advisor to employees and management alike, act like one. If you want to be treated like a disciplinarian or bureaucratic roadblock, act like one.

I was on a coaching call with Jack, the manager of his company's technical support department, when he said to me:

"I'm still trying to understand the culture here. Since I've only been here three months, I'm still learning about the people, the processes, and the customers. But some things are just different, and I don't understand why they are the way they are. Just yesterday, I happened to have a few minutes between customer calls, so I

decided to stop into Elliott's (the HR manager's) office. I haven't had any one-on-one time with him since I was hired, so I thought I'd see if he had time for a quick break too.

Anyway, he was kind enough to take a break, but he really didn't care about getting to know me any better. You know Elliott. He's not really an upbeat guy. He comes across like he's overburdened. Anyway, I left after just a few minutes. But then when I walked back into my department, two of my team members came to my office and asked, 'Why were you in Elliott's office? Is everything ok? You're not leaving are you?' When I explained I had just stopped in to get to know Elliott a bit better, they both asked,

'Why?' like it was a completely useless activity. Liz, it was weird. Am I weird for wanting to get to know the HR manager better?"

I had to assure him that what he was doing was great and not weird at all. It's just that this negative and punitive view of HR is pervasive. Because human resources departments have a tendency to be secretive about the collaborative work they do with others (see Chapter 3!), their roles are often misunderstood. Jack wanted to get to know his fellow managers better, which included Elliott, but Jack's team members assumed he was either in trouble or leaving the company. They'd seen other managers in Elliott's office, and those meetings rarely had happy endings. Being seen in the HR office wasn't viewed as a sign of a potential collaboration, it was viewed as a sign of a probable termination.

Executive teams and upper management have helped create and sustain this misperception. Because of their own misunderstandings of what human resources can and should do, their misunderstanding filters down into the rest of the organization. When leadership teams only call on HR to "handle" employee situations, they help perpetuate that negative stereotype.

The problem is that as human resources professionals, *you* need to take back your own image, because no one else can do that for you. Unfortunately, what I usually see is the HR department either retreating into itself or working feverishly to throw a festive employee morale boosting party. Neither activity is helpful in refining your image or changing the perception of your value. If you're typically delivering bad news or adding complicated paperwork and processes to your colleagues' plates, you can see why you and HR are branded negatively. It's time to take control of HR's image within your organization.

Here's what I suggest you do instead: Review the previous four chapters to get clearer yourself on the value of what you do, what your HR department does, what your HR team does and you could do to move your organization forward. Then identify how to more effectively demonstrate and communicate that to others within the organization.

Identify the ways and situations in which you may be branding HR as cumbersome, legalistic, punitive, or bureaucratic. Then adjust how you interact and communicate with others to change how they perceive you. Be approachable in spite of the regulations you have to adhere to. No one cares about the regulations. They care about how you treat them. A contributor, Suzanne

Welker, the former Vice President of Human Resources for Berger Hospital Systems, shared:

"Nurses have regulations to follow, but they don't say to their patients, 'Hello, I have to give you this antibiotic within six hours of your procedure or it reflects on our publically reported core measures. If that happens, it can impact the reputation of our hospital. Therefore, I have to follow the protocol; you have to take the antibiotic, or I may be at risk for moving into the first step of the disciplinary process.'

Identify the ways and situations in which you may be branding HR as cumbersome, legalistic, punitive, or bureaucratic.

Even though you have more people coming to your office to complain than most other departments, you need to keep in mind, that's what you want. That's your job. Your job is to help others *clear* their workplace roadblocks. To encourage people to come to you so you can partner with them and advise them on how to move forward, you need to be approachable.

Make eye contact in the moment, and write your notes later. Don't document, document,

document while someone is talking with you. It reinforces the notion you're bureaucratic and legalistic.

Quit whining to others about your workload and challenges. Everyone is busy. Besides, no one else cares and you come across as weak and ineffective.

Be accessible. More than any department, yours should have an open-door policy. You and your team should not be closed up behind locked doors and only accessible in short windows of time... with a secret handshake. Yes you need to protect the confidentiality of the information you process within your department, but you can do that in a way that is still open, welcoming, and professional.

Identify ways to minimize the paperwork and documentation. Find ways to help the managers and employees do things in easier, less time-consuming, and less bureaucratic ways.

Identify ways to minimize the paperwork and documentation. Find ways to help the managers and employees do things in easier, less time-consuming and less bureaucratic ways.

Finally, if you are in the unfortunate position of having inherited a negative HR brand from a prior HR manager or professional who did not serve that position well, you need to step-up in your rebranding efforts. It will take more time to reshape the perceptions of many within the organization, but it won't change if you don't start. The reality of the situation is that regardless of how you came into the position and regardless of the brand it had before you took it over, it is now your job, your department, and your position and brand to move forward. It's time to no longer keep what you do a secret. It's time to be an incredibly strong manager, clarify the value of what HR is and will be doing, and communicate that well.

Regardless of the brand the department had or has, it is now your job to ensure you are establishing and maintaining the right brand going forward.

"Your personal brand is what people say about you when you're not in the room."
— Chris Drucker, founder and CEO, Virtual Staff Finder

{ 6 } Stop Saying "No" or "You Can't" as a First Response

"I've given up on HR. I've learned to bypass them and go directly to the CEO, the COO, or VP of Operations. I'm not going to waste my time with HR."

— *Source Kept Confidential*

WHY: WHEN YOU typically say "no" or "you can't" as a first response to a manager's request, in the eyes of that manager, you're a big, bureaucratic roadblock. Now even though your answer was correct—the manager could not legally do what she was requesting—you're the bad guy. You see, the manager came to you for advice, for guidance, for direction, and for support in moving whatever the issue was—forward. So when your first response to her was "no," you were no longer viewed as a partner, advisor, or guide. You were viewed as a roadblock and a hindrance in helping her to do what she wanted to do. You made her life harder not easier. You also took the first fatal step to being branded as "legalistic, bureaucratic, and closed-minded." You're also quickly becoming someone (or a department) to avoid if at all possible.

Once this happens, word will spread quickly that HR is difficult to work with and is bureaucratic. That negative brand also often translates into an understanding by members of the management team that anything that's not already a clear precedent or an easy issue for HR to support, won't be approved or supported, so don't even bother asking. HR has limited creative abilities. They don't think creatively. They think like bureaucrats. Either work around them or don't do it. Just don't take it to them or they'll shut you down.

When you typically say "no" or "you can't" as a first response to a manager's request, in the eyes that manager, you're a big, bureaucratic roadblock.

On a coaching call with Kyle, the owner of a regional franchise, he said to me:

"It's a nightmare having to deal with Laura! Everything is so difficult and bureaucratic with her. It feels like a battle every time I have to talk with her about an employee issue. Hiring new employees has become a huge process. Reprimanding an employee now requires two managers' time in addition to the employee's time. Giving one of Robin's employees a raise created all kinds of work for Robin, and heaven

forbid, we try to fire an employee. Laura will probably tell us we need to jump through some new bureaucratic hoops we've never had to deal with before.

I told Laura yesterday, I think she's just making this all way more difficult than it needs to be. She didn't like it, but I'd had it with her. There's no doubt she knows HR law and all that stuff, but it's like she's working against us instead of with us. I'm considering just telling the rest of the management team to work around her. As the saying goes, It's easier to ask forgiveness than permission. *At least we'll be able to get some things done."*

This experience of Kyle's is all too common, and totally unproductive.

Here's what I suggest you do instead: Stop saying "no" or "you can't" as a first response when you know the managers can't legally do what they want to do. Stop being a roadblock. Start being a resource. Start to view situations like these for what they are—opportunities to help colleagues move forward. If the direct approach they had proposed isn't going to work, offer to use your expertise to help identify an alternative approach to move them towards their objective. Start by saying what you will do or what they could do. Imagine how different

Kyle's experience with HR would be if Laura said something like this:

"Let me do some research on how we might be able to make this - or something close to it - happen. I understand what you're trying to do, but the approach you're suggesting isn't possible because of our current contract with the insurance company. Why don't you put together a list of everyone you believe would be impacted by this, and I'll do some research on my end to see how we might make something like this work. Let's meet next week then to see what we can do."

If the direct approach they had proposed isn't going to work, offer to use your expertise to help identify an alternative approach to move them towards their objective.

Listen harder. Stop saying "no" or "you can't" as a first reply when what they're asking for isn't illegal (but would create a lot of work for you and others). Again, keep in mind this is an opportunity to help them, but it's also an opportunity for you to be creative. Instead of saying "no" and shutting them down, ask them to explain more fully what objectives they're trying to achieve and why. By listening more carefully to them, you may be able to identify a creative, less work-intensive solution.

Review your correspondence. Don't start your replies to emails or letters with "no" or "unfortunately." Partners, advisors, and leaders move people forward; they don't stonewall or block their people. Again, start by saying what you will do or have done; "I've included Bob Jackson our Director of Finance on this email. Bob will be able to ...."

Finally, start saying "yes" to requests to help with projects outside of your current skill-set. Be willing to take a risk, learn more, do more, be seen more, network more, and enhance your brand more.

Partners, advisors, and leaders move people forward; they don't stonewall or block their people.

"*Say 'yes,' and you'll figure it out afterwards.*"

— *Tina Fey, actress, writer, and producer*

{ 7 } Stop Giving Lip Service to Training and Coaching

"Maybe it's time to stop thinking about changing the way the world sees us and our profession, and to start to transform ourselves inside the profession."

— *Bette J. Francis, SPHR, 2014 Board Chair, Society for Human Resource Management*

WHY: IT'S EASY to spot a learning hypocrite. That's a person who claims to believe in continual learning and development, yet doesn't participate in training opportunities or work on self-development. It's also easy to respect someone who isn't perfect, yet seeks out and takes advantage of opportunities to learn and improve him or herself. Given these two options, which would your team and colleagues select that more closely describes you?

The idea for this chapter came from a few of the contributors to this book, who, not surprisingly, asked to remain anonymous. So here's the real point of this chapter: More than any other department, you have access to numerous training and coaching opportunities. Therefore, others expect that you would be modeling, using, and sharing what you have been exposed to—to some degree—through training. Others expect that you should be improving yourself and your skills on a regular basis. You should be developing as a manager—and as a person.

Others expect you to be modeling, using, and sharing what you have been exposed to—to some degree—through training.

Just by your association with an abundance of training, others expect you to be benefiting from it. Therefore, because you may be required to teach and train employees on various topics routinely, what have you extrapolated and used yourself or in HR? When you've had to source and then sit in on training sessions provided by others, what did you learn that you applied or shared with others? More importantly, how often did you take advantage of training targeted to someone like you, in your position, with issues you face?

Or, how often have you said, "I'm too busy to sit in on the training"? Here's the interesting part of that typical reply for me: By stating you're too busy to "sit in" on the training indicates you don't believe you have any need to actually attend as a participant with an open mind to learning. Your attendance would simply be for show. You'd sit there. You wouldn't really be there to learn.

We all have weaknesses and need to improve in some way shape or form. So as a professional representing a department and profession that touts the importance of training and development, when you're not open to learning yourself, your credibility and ability to influence others diminishes.

As the Deputy Director for Workforce Readiness, Diane had a large portfolio of responsibilities, projects, and team members to manage. She also had a tendency to be so busy being busy, she didn't have time to actively participate in executive level training herself, nor did she observe or fully appreciate any programs her staff created or presented. As a result, one of her program directors shared with me after a leadership training session that Diane had again failed to attend:

"You know Liz, I understand she's busy. But for goodness sakes, she could show some support for what we do. Besides, she might even learn something. Goodness knows, she could use some stronger time and team management skills."

By chance that afternoon, I had a coaching meeting with Diane. As soon as I walked into her office, Diane immediately acknowledged the fact that she'd not been at that morning's session. However, she rationalized that her schedule was "just too full to sit in yet another program that had nothing new to offer" her. I couldn't help myself, so I had to ask her, "Diane, why do you have so much more to do than your six managers who were in this morning's session?"

I again let her rationalize how demanding of her time her boss was, but it quickly became apparent to Diane and to me that she wasn't managing herself, her time, her boss, or her team well. Diane stopped talking, took a deep breath, looked at me and then started again:

"Oh God, I've become that hypocrite manager you talk about haven't I? Liz, I know

this stuff, but I've forgotten to intentionally apply it." She sighed and then sat back in her chair and talked more to herself than to me. *"I need to do this for myself and my team. I need to take time for training, if for nothing else, to simply listen for that one nugget of insight that will help me at that moment."*

Here's what I suggest you do instead: Be a role model by admitting you are not perfect and you need to take time for learning too. If you can't model the importance of continuing to learn, grow, and develop yourself, don't expect other managers or your employees to jump at the chance to develop themselves either—no matter how badly they may need it. The greatest success my company has in helping leadership teams change an organization's culture is when the most senior person (the president, CEO, owner, or executive director) says honestly to the entire leadership team, "I know I'm not perfect, and I need to learn as much if not more than you." Then models program after program his or her dedication to learning, a willingness to try new techniques, and the humor and humility to say, "I'm still not good at X, but I'm working on it!"

If you don't model the importance of continuing to learn, grow, and develop yourself, don't expect other managers or your employees to jump at the chance to develop themselves either—no matter how badly they may need it.

Stop allowing your technical and analytical skills to be "OK" instead of "Good" or "Ahead of the Curve." From a purely practical perspective, given the rapid changes in regulations, HR support software applications, industry shifts, economic, and employment demographic trends, and so on, if you're not actively working to stay current and abreast of what's happening, you'll quickly be out of touch and ill-equipped to do your job.

The growing prominence of workforce analytics software and services alone is just one area of education and training you need to be actively engaged in or you will soon be struggling to catch up. You don't need to become a master of workforce analytics, but you need to understand what they are, what they can do for your organization, how you might use them to support leadership and business decisions. At a bare minimum, you need to get much quicker and better at extracting the right data from the workforce analytics you've already got or which are available to you, and synthesize it into usable formats for the leadership team to use in decision-making. If you don't know how use your current workforce analytics data, get training by your Human Resources System (HRS) software provider or a certified consultant or trainer on workforce analytics.

To reiterate thoughts shared in Chapter 4, learn to speak the financial language of your business. Either take classes on business finances, or simply spend dedicated time with the CFO or other finance team members to learn more about your organization's finances, your department's finances, and the impact various employee actions and business decisions have on them.

If you're not actively working to stay current and abreast of what's happening, you'll quickly be out of touch and ill-equipped to do your job

Also, look at making training more impactful for others, not only yourself. Ensure all managers know how to coach their employees to better performance. Position HR to be the place where you teach your managers to teach and you coach the managers on coaching their employees. Then ensure you participate in the learning and model how it's done.

Finally, participating in many of the training programs, seminars, or coaching opportunities presented to you may not be helpful or a good use of your time. I realize that, and I fully realize they take time away from an already packed schedule. However, for your colleagues who are ambivalent about them, when you demonstrate the importance of making time, participating in targeted offerings, and applying what you learn, colleagues tend to resist less and participate more. Besides, you never know when you might hear that nugget of insight you need to enable you to become more effective.

You never know when you might hear that nugget of insight you need to enable you to become more effective.

"Before companies can upskill their workforces and leadership, they must upskill HR."

— Chris Groscurth and Ryan Ott, authors, "Strengthening HR to Meet Global Business Demands," *Gallup Business Journal*, February 26, 2015

{ 8 } Stop Acting Like a Cost Center Instead of a Value Center

"The sad fact is that in most organizations, HR is denied spending requests perhaps more than any other function."

— *Jeff Higgins, author, "Bringing HR and Finance Together with Analytics," HR Magazine, Nov 2014*

WHY: WHEN YOU perceive your own department as a cost center, you behave as such. If you believe and act as a cost center, you'll be treated as such. Cost centers are monitored and controlled. They're not typically allowed to grow. In fact, they're often studied to determine ways to reduce them.

Cost centers are monitored and controlled. They're not typically allowed to grow.

Granted, your organization's human resources expenditures may well be your organization's largest expense. However, don't behave as if it's your fault or a bad thing. If the human resources expenditures are a significant if not the largest expense area of your organization, that only increases your obligation to not behave as a cost center, but rather as an asset management and investment center.

How often have you heard or said yourself, "Our employees are our most valuable asset"? If your employees are the organization's most valuable asset, then your role is that of not only managing numerous aspects of the most valuable assets' experiences while with your organization, but also to ensure the managers are best utilizing, leveraging, supporting, developing, investing in, and protecting your organization's most valuable assets too. Like most assets, to operate optimally over time, your employees need to be properly cared for and reinvested in to ensure their on-going productivity.

When you view your role as one that best leverages the assets your company has instead of simply how to cut costs, you start to analyze potential cash outlays differently and your expectations of performance become clearer. Instead of simply seeing a potential personnel related-expense that would *hopefully* provide some benefit, you analyze the proposed expense to more clearly understand the potential impact on your employees and the desired performance change because of that impact. You become much clearer on the value of each expense and are better able to either justify an expense or dismiss it as not capable of producing a strong enough return on investment.

Behave as an asset management and investment center, not a cost center.

I was consulting with Ryan, a bank's Regional Manager of Human Resources, when he looked at me and said:

"I don't think Joe will give us the money for this. I like what you've included in your proposal. It's exactly what we need. But this is more than he was anticipating. I know he's concerned with how he would have to justify this

type of expense to the board, and this is more than what he was expecting."

Ryan had called me the week before and asked my company to help him create an ongoing leadership training program for the bank that could be used across all levels of management from front-line supervisors to senior staff. The program would focus on creating more consistent, solid management terminology and skills across all departments, branches, and throughout all layers of leadership. In particular, the first year's topics would be sequenced to address their managers' most important learning needs first to minimize further egregious management missteps.

The program was specifically designed this way, because Ryan and the other managers, with whom I had met, had referenced various examples of mismanaged personnel actions within the past year that had caused legal issues for the bank, had negatively impacted morale, and had lost the bank one large valued account.

"Ryan," I asked, "do you believe this program will address the issues you shared with me last week?"

"Yes I do," he replied.

"Then all we need to do is explain to Joe the value of this investment. By implementing this program, he'll greatly reduce the likelihood of future costly personnel actions like you've experienced this past year. This program is less than the cost of just two of those actions."

"That's true," Ryan replied.

I continued, "And here's another way to look at how and where to best invest the bank's monies: How much do you think the bank is spending on the new landscaping and signage at your branches this year?"

Ryan looked at me confused. "I don't know. I know it's part of the expansion plan!"

I replied, "What do you think is more important to helping Joe and the board hit the bank's targeted KPIs (Key Performance Indicators) this year: updated landscaping and signage or a well-trained management team?"

Ryan looked at me and said, "Let's go talk to Joe." We did and the project moved forward.

I share this story with you so you can ask yourself: Do I clarify and justify the value of investing in initiatives I propose, or do I present the initiatives as expenses?

Do I clarify and justify the value of investing in initiatives I propose, or do I present the initiatives as expenses?

Here's what I suggest you do instead: Reframe your thinking of HR-related costs so they become investments in assets rather than expenses. When you need to present initiatives for approval, sell the benefits: moving the organization forward, helping to hit a targeted KPI, enhancing asset value, increasing ROI, reducing waste, increasing productive time, etc. As you get better at clarifying and presenting your proposed initiatives this way, you'll notice that you have an easier time getting your ideas approved, costly or not. You have to learn to negotiate and build a case. Negotiate as hard for your initiatives as you do for another leader's. Learn to build a case and give a focused, value-driven, data-driven rationale.

Be consistent and clear in that all HR decisions are based upon the strategic plan, which drives all HR plans, including all succession and workforce plans. You're simply trying to identify ways to ensure the company has the right workforce, with the right skills, at the right time. By learning to use objective data and science rather than subjective opinions, you'll make stronger points, and again, increase your chances of having your initiatives approved.

Along those same lines, tie your HR initiatives and negotiating points to the organization's Key Performance Indicators (KPIs) whenever possible. You'll have much stronger justification for your actions when you can show their positive impact on the KPIs. All key initiatives (driven by HR or other departments) should tie to the KPIs, which should tie to the organization's strategic plan.

Calculate and more clearly explain the potential for cost savings and greater return on investment (ROI) for HR initiatives and programs. Refer to the exercise in Chapter 3, and calculate the estimated dollar value of the benefits your work and/or initiatives have brought to the organization. To do this, you need to determine how the activity had a financial impact. Did the activity positively or negatively impact personnel hours and costs, legal costs, production-related costs, and so on. Then calculate the size of the impact or dollar amount.

A CEO once asked me how he would benefit by personally participating in the proposed leadership training. I shared with him:

"Well, you stated earlier that one of your personal reasons for even considering this type of training is that you would like your managers to be more effective during the week, so you're not personally here every Saturday doing things that didn't get done during the week. So let's keep this simple and assume you work eight hours every Saturday. That's roughly 32 additional hours each month you're here and not with your family. If the training helped your managers gain stronger skills so you would only

have to spend 16 but better yet, no weekend hours here each month. Would it be worth it?"

His eyes started to glimmer a bit, and he said, "Yeah I guess it would."

"Now here's another way of looking at that same scenario: If you're currently spending an average of 32 hours each month, at your loaded hourly rate, doing work your managers should be doing or did incorrectly, how expensive are those tasks now becoming?"

He smiled, and said, "You've made your point. Let's do this."

Be ready to answer specific questions such as: What has been the financial impact of the training you provided to managers on better new-hire, on-boarding training? How has that training helped to impact the historical costs of probationary employee terminations, negative employee actions, and ramp-up time to achieve expected productivity levels, productivity waste, safety, and innovation? If you don't know, this is a great exercise to ask the accounting or finance manager to help you calculate.

You need to be able to demonstrate not only the morale and culture-enhancing aspects of what you do, but the financial impact as well. Be able to share things such as, "With the enhanced training, we now see the new hires' productive ramp up time at 2.5 weeks versus a traditional 6-7 weeks. This means the average hourly production employee is generating work at fully expected rates roughly 3.5-4 weeks earlier than we've ever seen before."

Make it easy for others with to say "yes" to your initiatives. Clarify the bottom-line ROI for moving forward. For example, by investing $250,000 in training, you could achieve a positive impact of $550,000 as a result of fewer employee legal actions, reduced turnover, and increases in account retention. What CEO or CFO is going to say "no" to that?

Create an HR Dashboard to share relevant data that ties into company/leadership KPIs. Capture and synthesize data you already have or can capture from your HR systems and third party HR vendors to present to the leadership team in financial, data-driven terms they'll understand, appreciate, and act upon:

- What is the cost of your current workforce compared to the workforce you'll need as you project where your organization wants to be in 3, 4, 5+ years, per your strategic plan?
- What is the cost of recruiting, hiring, onboarding, training, coaching and retaining right-fit employees versus quick-fit employees that don't produce, cause personnel actions, and waste management time?

- What is the cost and production impact of no-to-limited (insert specific type of training here) training and cross-training?
- What is the cost and production impact of no-to-limited emergency staffing and workforce planning?
- What is the cost and production impact when select employees, who have no identified back-up person or persons, are away from work?
- What will be the cost and production impact if the projected retirees do leave within the next 3-5 years and others have not been cross-trained in those areas?

Remember—and I can't say this enough—learn to speak in numbers. Learn how the other departments make and spend money. How do they measure ROI? What are their headache areas concerning production, finances, and everything else? How do employees and performance impact their areas of focus? Start to think like a CFO to appreciate the sensitivity of the numbers and how many leaders manage-by-the-numbers.

Finally, learn by working alongside others. Team up with the production or operations manager as well as with the CFO on a few projects to better understand their key trigger issues, their terminology, their worlds, their worries, and their responsibilities. Learn about them and their influence on the organization so you're better prepared to negotiate with them and influence them and their decision-making processes.

Reframe your thinking of HR-related costs from expenses to investing in assets, enhancing asset value, and increasing ROI.

"I always did something I was a little not ready to do. I think that's how you grow. When there's that moment of, 'Wow, I'm not really sure I can do this,' and you push through those moments, that's when you have a breakthrough."

— *Marissa Mayer, CEO, Yahoo.*

{ 9 } Stop Being a Weak Manager Yourself

"By the way, when you find cracking HR leaders, hold on to them for dear life. They are as rare as hen's teeth."

— Peter Flade, Jim Harter, and Jim Asplund, authors, "Seven Things Great Employers Do (That Others Don't)," Gallup Business Journal, April 15, 2014

WHY: WHEN YOU yourself do not model effective, strong, and consistent management and leadership skills, you are in no position to comment on or advise members of the leadership team on how to be better managers or leaders. You need to be the model of how "leadership is done."

Most basically, effective HR managers apply what they've learned or should have learned through experience and in the various training and coaching programs they've helped bring in-house or have participated in elsewhere. These managers read the environment and manage themselves accordingly so they can best interact with and support the leadership team and environment.

Also let's be honest, it's terribly irritating working with or working for a manager who can't manage. If you don't plan and manage projects well, you're not modeling strong management skills. If you don't respond in a timely fashion to text messages, phone calls, emails, and other communication requests, you're not modeling strong management skills. If you don't have a team or systems in place to take care of things while you're away or unavailable, you're not modeling strong management skills. And if you don't have other managers coming to you and asking for your advice on how they can be better managers, you're not modeling strong HR management skills. In a nutshell, you're not doing your job.

Solid human resources professionals and managers apply many of the insights they've internalized during their personal and working interactions and experiences, as well as in various training opportunities. They've also taken the initiative to collaborate with other departments to understand the business and clarify how HR can best help the other managers and the leadership team move the company forward.

Solid HR managers also are keenly aware of how every business decision effects personnel in some way shape or form; therefore, they need to be keenly aware of the business issues being discussed and decided. HR understands they can impact strategy, culture, performance, and finances. Because of this, according to an article in the Spring 2014 issue of Korn Ferry's *Briefings Magazine*, talented HR executives are fast becoming highly recruited targets for board leadership positions. Though corporate CEOs are the most-recruited group for board and corporate board positions, strong HR executives are also targeted.

Bob Hallagan, Vice Chairman and Managing Director of Board Leadership Services at Korn Ferry International shared, "Ensuring a company has the right CEO leadership and an environment that attracts top talent is a key driver in shareholder value..., and HR executives can certainly add value."

Per Peter Flade, Jim Harter, and Jim Asplund in their article, "Seven Things Great Employers Do (That Others Don't)" from the April 15, 2014 issue of the *Gallup Business Journal*, "The best HR people have a gift for influencing, teaching and holding executives accountable. This is important because many executives rise through the ranks despite not being very good managers."

And this is not just the opinion of a few people. In a 2014 study for the *Harvard Business Review*, titled "Talent: Why Chief Human Resources Officers Make Great CEOs," Ellie Filler, senior client partner of executive recruiting firm Korn Ferry and University of Michigan professor Dave Ulrich explore this idea in detail. According to Ulrich, "great CHROs [Chief Human Resource Officers] are very highly paid because they're very hard to find."

In fact, Filler and Ulrich believe great CHROs are so rare, that after CEOs and COOs, they are typically the third highest-paid executives within an organization. Their study also revealed that the executives with traits most similar to those of the CEO were the COO and the CHRO. They came to the conclusion that more companies should consider CHROs when looking to fill CEO positions; however, CHROs need broad business exposure to be CEO material, which means they need to branch out from the HR world. They need to acquire technical and financial skills, learn the business, speak the language of finance, and learn to function across diverse areas like a CEO does.

I was packing up after a work session, when I heard someone say, *"I wanted to say good-bye."* I looked up from my client's strategic planning file to see Renee, an HR team member, standing by the conference room door.

"Hey! Thanks for stopping and thanks for your help in setting everything up for today. How have you been?" I replied.

"Oh I'm great!" Renee responded. *"Tomorrow is my last day. I'm leaving!"*

"Really? Is this change something you wanted?"

"Oh, yeah. I needed to save my sanity. I couldn't take it anymore."

"What do you mean?"

"Liz, Karen is so good at making the leadership team think she's a great manager, they believe her and don't pay attention to what really happens in HR. If they knew what she was really like as a manager, they'd be amazed. Did you know, HR has the highest turnover rate of any department? It's true and it's not because we're being promoted or going to other

departments here. We're leaving to get away from her! She's a nice person, but she's a horrible manager!

The reason Karen works such long hours isn't because she's got such important things to do, it's because she won't address the drama and personnel issues within her own department and she's so disorganized! It's pathetic actually. Anyway, I've had enough. I gave her my two week's notice and she didn't seem surprised. I guess it's become her reality that her team members leave, but she doesn't seem to realize she's the problem. What's that tell you about our HR Director and the quality of the HR Department?"

Ouch. Let's make sure no one can say anything remotely close to this about you.

Here's what I suggest you do instead: Use your emotional intelligence, your situational awareness, and your understanding of personality types to interact effectively with your colleagues, team members, other employees, contractors, customers, and vendors alike.

Model how effective leaders communicate. Deal with conflicts, difficult situations, and problems assertively and transparently. Don't get stuck in text or email loops. Get up and talk with people or pick up the phone.

Learn to rock at project management. Be organized. Get comfortable at holding team members, consultants, vendors and others accountable. These skills are the cornerstones of strong management. This is how you build respect and move towards the next levels of responsibility.

Focus on the future. Focus on building depth within your team, department, and organization with a deep and wide pool of well-skilled, and highly engaged employees. In other words, support your team first and put into play various programs, processes, and systems that are simple yet consistent in what they're intended to achieve. Great teams with well-trained employees are built over time, and it is your job to back up the efforts that will get your team to this goal.

As an HR manager was told after her first leadership team staff meeting, "get bigger shoulders," and learn to hold your own with the other managers. Don't take it personally when you've been circumvented or your opinion has been rejected. Take it professionally and identify why the idea failed. Build a stronger case the next time.

For tips on how to be a better manager and leader, read my book: Something Needs to Change Around Here - The Five Stages to Leveraging Your Leadership. You'll gain insights into developing your management and leadership skills, supporting your team more effectively, and an understanding of how to leverage your team to get what you need done.

Finally, work to build a portfolio of successes. You want to be able to show that regardless of the team or project you're responsible for, you build that team or project team into a solid functioning unit that is effective without you being around. Where ever you go or with whatever project team you lead, demonstrate how to build a solid team that is self-sufficient. Demonstrate your value throughout the organization as you help troubleshoot situations and areas that need solid leadership and solid management.

> *"How would the person I'd like to be do the thing I'm about to do?"*
>
> *— Jim Cathcart, author, speaker, and leadership expert*

{ 10 } Stop Thinking You Can't Drive the Big Initiatives

"I learned to always take on things I'd never done before. Growth and comfort do not coexist."

Ginni Rometty, CEO, IBM

WHY: YOU NEVER know you can do it until you try, and you won't be viewed as an effective leader, partner, or advisor until you do.

If you let your own fears or the incorrect perceptions of others hold you back from trying to do what you believe needs to be done to move the organization forward, stop complaining about your job or your organization. You've given up your right to complain because you've accepted the labels and misperceptions of others. You also might as well accept that your lot in life is to just show up and do what's in front of you. If you want to make a difference, you've got to have the self-confidence and courage to take risks and do what's never been done in your organization before.

If you want to make a difference, you've got to have the self-confidence and courage to take risks and do what's never been done in your organization before.

As I shared in Chapter 1, as Heidi shifted her mindset of her position and the important role she needed to better fulfill, she started to behave differently. Heidi pushed for select initiatives. She saw a clear need to strengthen the leadership team's skills. Heidi believed they, as a leadership team needed to not only became more functional, but they also needed to enhance their basic management skills. They needed to better support their employees and they needed to move quickly to eliminate numerous one-deep scenarios throughout the organization. When Heidi raised the need to address these issues, not surprisingly she was told, "If you think they're important, then you make them happen." She did.

If you think they're important, then you make them happen.

Over a three-year timeframe, Heidi proposed, justified, gained approval for, and spearheaded several major workforce initiatives.

Her initiatives have changed the culture, enhanced communication, caused departmental reorganizations and position adjustments, minimized one-deep scenarios, increased collaboration, reduced waste and down time, enhanced the interviewing and on-boarding process, and created a much more transparent culture with clear expectations. Heidi served as project manager to bring in comprehensive leadership training for the entire management and supervisory team, along with access to on-line training 24/7. Continuity and access to the new leadership concepts for current and new managers was critical.

Heidi led the initiative to conduct on-going, comprehensive succession planning and workforce mapping with the leadership team. They needed to uncover and target one-deep scenarios to minimize production disruptions and enhance skills across the production floor. As this project took hold, it positioned Heidi to lead a management task force to complete a review and rewrite all of the position descriptions to enhance clarity, standards, and expectations. As this project neared completion, Heidi pushed forward the next phase of change: introducing a revamped and integrated performance management process and format that would tie all workforce initiatives and personnel documents together.

Heidi again served as project manager for all document updates, training and calibration work sessions. By collaborating with the Technical Services Manager, Heidi created an easy, one-stop-shop reporting tool for all managers.

Needless to say, none of these initiatives were easy or quick. Heidi had to negotiate, prod, remind, take charge, challenge, ask, and often just wait, but she didn't give up. It took three years, but Heidi's actions and successes caused the other managers to view and treat her differently. They now look to her as not only a respected peer, but also as an advisor and partner in moving the company forward. When Heidi raises issues concerning the business, the leadership team, or the workforce, the leadership team listens. Heidi's now highly effective—and respected.

Here's what I suggest you do instead: Believe in yourself and do what you know needs to be done.

In a February 26, 2015 article in *Gallup Business Journal,* authors Chris Groscurth and Bryant Ott, said, "No one is questioning whether companies need better human development strategies to improve leadership and drive business growth and performance. Instead, the issue is how to redefine the role HR plays..."

The issue is how to redefine the role HR plays in supporting business performance.

From my experience, initiating an organizational change and many personnel-related policy changes takes, on average, three years. In that time period, you're introducing and selling the idea to others, pulling your team together, building the team and managing their personalities, working through the project, making adjustments, working out the kinks, communicating with stakeholders to minimize resistance, introducing the project to the end-users, addressing push-back and making further adjustments, going live with the new process, and then determining how to ensure the new process and its benefits stick. None of this is easy, but it's what great managers do.

Believe in yourself and do what you know needs to be done.

Don't think you have to do any of this alone. Develop trusted relationships with other managers. Identify and intentionally engage in conversations and debates with members of the management team to identify who will engage with you, challenge you, and allow you to challenge them for the good of the organization. This also helps you to determine who to work with and how on future projects.

Initiate collaborative projects with other department managers to help move initiatives forward—yours, theirs, and the organization's. You need to know the entire business so you can best support all managers in helping them move their departments forward. To do that, you need to understand their worlds too, not just HR's.

Recognize and leverage the effectiveness of using office politics to advance the organization's mission. In order to become a respected partner and advisor, you need to get things done, you need to know who to go to in order to get things done, and you need to be able to have established a relationship with others so they will help you. This is how I define office politics: It's knowing who to go to get things done. Office politics is working your network; it's not catty gossip.

Focus the leadership team on what solid leadership planning means: It's ensuring that you've created an organization with a clear vision, have identified the organizational structure to support that vision, and know the types of positions and talents needed to support, manage, and lead that type of organization. It's ensuring you've helped develop a leadership team that works with you, HR, to ensure you can help them have the right people, in the right place, with the right skills, at the right time, within an environment that attracts and retains good-fit employees.

To do that, I suggest you be the champion of several intentional, strategic initiatives:

Create an organization that believes in solid leadership development and succession planning:

- Ensure the strategic plan is solid and focused.
- Analyze the strategic plan to clearly understand where the organization is headed in the next 3, 4, 5+ years.
- Talk with the managers to review your organizational chart to identify current Hot Spots (i.e., one-deep scenarios).
- Identify gaps in *current* resources (people, skills, knowledge, etc.) and those needed to effectively *achieve the vision*.
- Work with the leadership team and plot your organizational chart, as it will be at your organization's vision state to

identify potential changes in staffing (new, eliminations, outsourcing, etc.)

- Hold one-on-one meetings with managers to discuss the needed changes to their departments and team members/positions.

- Teach managers and supervisors to identify talent and develop their employees, as well as how to regularly discuss performance with staff. Teach managers how to hold Necessary Conversations.

- Work with the managers to create position descriptions for positions needed in the future. Determine needed knowledge, skills, behaviors, values, and assess those against current position descriptions. Focus position descriptions on results not tasks.

- Revise the Performance Review Process and Compensations Plans if necessary.
- Provide training to staff to clarify how and why the changes are occurring and what the future, fully-accountable and learning organization will look like.
- Create clear, comprehensive training and development plans for the organization and individuals. Focus on the Emergency Staffing Plan and the Hot Spots first, then

move to other areas and future workforce needs.

- Provide or source targeted, comprehensive leadership training for all levels of management to promote consistency of practice and vocabulary.
- Create and facilitate a management development team to continually identify employees demonstrating Stage 1, 2, 3, 4, or 5 Leadership potential and trust them with more appropriate responsibilities.
- Develop mentoring programs (i.e., young to older and experienced to less-experienced) for experiential interactions

and learning, while encouraging informal mentoring.

- Enable shadowing, cross-training and cross-departmental learning; structured job rotation if possible, if not, basic awareness and overview sessions of organization-wide activities, successes, and challenges.

- Review the Succession and Workforce Plans annually with the leadership team to ensure they continue to support the strategic plan as it is updated.

- Create applications-oriented training opportunities in conjunction with business units, i.e., special projects, committees, task forces, etc.

- Drive the creation of a culture of learning and development.
- Hold everyone accountable to grow as their positions evolve to support the organization as it moves forward.
- Be confident and model what it means to be a partner and key advisor to the leadership team.

You never know you can until you try, and you won't be viewed as an effective leader, partner, or advisor until you do.

"Be the change you wish to see."

— Mahatma Gandhi, Indian Independence Movement Leader

Conclusion

"Some people today are wandering generalities instead of meaningful specifics because they have failed to discover and mine the wealth of potentials in them."

— *Ifeanyi Enoch Onuoha, Educator*

THIS BOOK WAS written to expand upon a speech I provide to HR groups frequently, *Become the Strategic Business Partner Your Team Needs!* I started giving the speech because in the 20+ years I've been working with organizations on succession planning and leadership development, there have only been two incidences in which the senior human resources professional has been named as a possible successor to the CEO. With each of these organizations and their respective leadership teams, it was also immediately apparent to me the senior human resources representative was respected as a key critical advisor not only to the President or CEO, but to the entire leadership team. It's happened only two times. Two.

Sadly, in my experience, more often than not, the weakest manager sitting at the leadership table is the human resources representative. (My belief as to some of the causes for this lie in the preceding chapters.) That needs to stop and stop now.

As a human resources professional you've got too much insight and expertise to sit idly by. If you've got a respected seat at the leadership and strategic planning table, make good use of it. Play your cards with intent so you can demonstrate how what you do adds value to the business. Advise the leadership team proactively to support stronger decision-making. Advocate for the employees when appropriate to strengthen your organization's human capital investment, and when it's the right thing to do.

The employees need you to do a few things differently. The managers need you to do a few things differently, and the leadership team needs you to do a few things differently. The few suggestions contained on these pages were shared to help you so you can better help them. What you do for your organization and the people who have the privilege of working with you is so important. What you can share to develop incredible teams, organizations, and shape organizational cultures is astounding. I hope my thoughts have helped you in a small way.

As I close, I want to extend a special thanks again to the over 300 human resources professionals I connected with in confirming many of my ideas for the book, and for sharing a few I hadn't yet considered. Needless to say, your insights on how to best help your peers count more than mine.

With that, I'll close this book by saying:

Thank you for taking on one of the most important roles in any organization. Now, ask yourself: Is there anything that I need to stop doing?

Continue Your Leadership Journey

Available at WBSLLC.com/Store

SOMETHING NEEDS TO CHANGE AROUND HERE
The Five Stages to Leveraging Your Leadership

- Are you tired of working 50, 60, 70 or more hours a week?
- Are you frustrated by what your team members don't do and can't figure out for themselves?
- Do you come in early and stay late just so you can get things done?
- Would you like to get your life back?

IF YOU ANSWERED YES TO EVEN ONE OF THESE QUESTIONS, YOU NEED THIS BOOK!

If you walk around complaining about your team or muttering to yourself, "Something needs to change around here," you're right. And it's probably you.

DON'T LET 'EM TREAT YOU LIKE A GIRL® — A WOMAN'S GUIDE TO LEADERSHIP SUCCESS

With insights gathered from women and men in leadership roles, Liz shares tips to help aspiring to experienced women leaders.

This quick-reading, insightful guide helps you identify:

- Which leadership traits are most admired
- What your leadership brand is saying about you
- How to manage conflicts and negotiations more effectively
- What "girly" behaviors you need to STOP!

This is a great resource for Women's Leadership programs!

Liz provides content-rich, interactive, skill-building presentations to groups large and small. Liz is known for her candor and her ability to customize her topics to meet your group's specific needs.

For more information, call +1(717)597.8890 or go to www.WBSLLC.com

About Liz Weber, CMC, CSP

In the words of one client, *"Liz Weber will help you see opportunities you never knew existed."*

Known for her candor, clear insights and straightforward approach, Liz Weber is a **sought-after management consultant, keynote speaker and seminar presenter**. She is one of fewer than 100 people in the U.S. to hold both the Certified Speaking Professional (CSP) and Certified Management Consultant (CMC) designations—the **highest earned designations in two different professions**.

As experts in strategic planning, succession planning and leadership development, Liz and her team are based near Harrisburg, Pennsylvania, and work with leaders to take their organizations:

- From no business strategy to enterprise-wide focus and clarity

- From no succession or workforce plan to enterprise-wide depth
- From a weak leadership team to a respected leadership team

Liz has supervised business activities in 129 countries and has consulted with organizations in over 20 countries. She has designed and facilitated conferences from Bangkok to Bonn and Tokyo to Tunis. Liz has taught for the Johns Hopkins University's Graduate School of Continuing Studies, as well as the Georgetown University's Senior Executive Leadership Program.

Liz is also the author of several leadership publications including:

- Something Needs to Change Around Here: The Five Stages to Leveraging Your Leadership
- Don't Let 'Em Treat You Like a Girl: A Woman's Guide to Leadership Success

- Stop So You Can Get The Results You Want

Liz's Manager's Corner column appears monthly in several trade publications, association newsletters, and internet resource centers for executives.

www.ingramcontent.com/pod-product-compliance
Lightning Source LLC
LaVergne TN
LVHW020927090426
835512LV00020B/3240